Spiritual Protection

for those who find themselves in dark places

Lori Phillips

ISBN: 0985417552
ISBN-13: 978-0985417550

This book is dedicated to all the souls ever created, those whose curiosity leads them unwittingly up against forces unknown, those who must venture into dark places to retrieve the lost, and those who must themselves climb out of darkness.

And to our Creator of Love.

"We are going to link up, hold hands, and walk out of hell together."

~ Mellen-Thomas Benedict

CONTENTS

ACKNOWLEDGMENTS

I would be remiss not to begin and end my acknowledgments without giving thanks and paying homage to God, the Alpha and the Omega, the Almighty, the Creator, the Eternal Father. However you care to define Him, or Her, we can agree that there is a Universal Source of Intelligence from which springs all of human wisdom. I am but a vessel, a conduit, a particle in this ever-expanding existence. I feel His Spirit within me. He is love.

I am eternally thankful also to all our soul siblings, those alive and passed, who contributed to my knowledge base of spiritual matters from world religions to New Age thinkers. To the psychics, ghost hunters, and theoretical physicists. (I laugh to think the last so named will cringe to be found in the same grouping!) No matter where you are on the spectrum of all that is, you are a part of all that is, and you have added to my understanding.

Thank you to my darling husband and children who have gone down strange paths with me as I quested for spiritual knowledge. Their love and devotion keep me strong and safe. My love for you transcends words.

To Lisa Shea, Yvonnie Boise, Jilly Florio, Deanna Joseph, Karen Elleise, Lauren D'Silva, Terri Johansen, Ian Edwards, Tuculia Washington, Debbie Grejdus, Susan Kraemer and all the editors at Bellaonline.com who have been a tremendous support to me as I continued to write about all I experience without judgment. You inspire and humble me. I love you all.

And to Becky Reed, Lena Suno and all those who inquired of me as they set out to fulfill their spiritual callings with their psychic gifts. They were the inspiration for this book on spiritual protection as I so wanted them to be prepared for their new journeys that may take them into dark places.

May you remember that love *is* the light.

"In this infinite universe, I am but a tiny speck. But I am a thankful speck, radiating love for all I'm worth." ~ Lori Phillips

INTRODUCTION

It was hard for me to balance this information for those who are completely new to spiritual matters and for those who are knowledgeable but still could use some additional information about spiritual protection. Please bear with me if you are on either extreme end of this vast belief spectrum! Even if you cannot accept some initial concepts, there will be some important thoughts later in the book that could serve you well at a most opportune time.

I will not get into debate over existential matters. You believe what you choose to believe. My purpose is not to convince you to abandon yours or convert to my beliefs about the reality of all things, the afterlife and beyond. But if you picked up this book, I will assume that you must have at least the very basic understanding that we humans are comprised of more than our physical mind and body but also our spirit.

It also will help make these matters easier to comprehend, if you understand that energy influences everything. Everything is made of energy vibrations. That might be more difficult to grasp, but I encourage you to read more about quantum physics as the field is discovering through electron microscopes that at the very particle level, all electrons vibrate. And it is at what speed that determines how this energy manifests. Whether a rock or water or an elephant or a color or a sound or even a human being. Everything is a beautiful, wondrous orchestration of vibrations!

Why is this so important to know? Because energy is everything. And, everything is energy. You will learn how to detect negative spirits by the energy they project. And you will learn how to *direct* yours and *draw upon divine sources of energy* to protect yourself.

If you're getting into ghost hunting or paranormal investigation as a hobby, I implore you to read this book in its entirety before you set out. If you're beginning to develop your psychic abilities, study the tarot or other divination tool, practice any type of metaphysical field, I honestly believe that this information can only strengthen you and your abilities to discern the spirit world while offering you methods of protection.

But even the average person who never venture anywhere near such activities can stumble into the path of unsettling, frightening, and even threatening energies. A haunted house. Wandering spirits. Residual energies in buildings or land. Accidentally opening energy portals through which negativity enters. Becoming the target of ill-intentioned folk. For him, this book can remove fear, restore your power and relieve you of unwanted spiritual interference.

About the religious overtones and terminology

There is nothing more polarizing than religion, and I certainly do not want to lose readers who might be non-religious *or* religious! As for my own personal religious stance, I consider myself omni-denominational. That is, I hold profound respect for all religions that attempt to seek the true God and help its adherents or followers elevate their understanding in a positive way. My understanding now is that every religion serves a purpose for its people, and there are unnecessary conflicts over semantics and misunderstanding.

To some, God is a personage; to others, a nebulous, omnipresent field of energy. I will not attempt to change how you believe. But do not be turned off if I use certain terminology that conflicts with your understanding. Please feel the spirit (energy) of my words.

As you proceed on your spiritual journey and should it take you down dark byways, remember your light of love and positive energy (divinity), for that will counter the darkness of negativity (evil). It matters less about the outward effects you use (rituals, worship) and more about the positive energy vibration you emanate (your feelings and spirit).

However, in this book, I do point out religious references but only to illustrate a point. I'm certain that if I searched different religious texts, there would be found similar references and understandings. Because of where I am, who I am and from where I came, I adhere to the belief of the Christ consciousness which is love. If you do not, please do not confuse this consciousness with the image and myth that man has made of the Christ.

There are some dimensions where there is not polarity, no duality as there is here on this physical plane of opposites. There, perhaps, true evil and goodness do not exist as we perceive them here. But because we are here in this time and space, and there is a duality of good and evil, it is key to combat negative and dark forces by their opposites which are positivity and light. Some people may be able to tap those energy forces without invoking the Christ consciousness through their own light, but I find it infinitely easier, faster and more sure to call upon the pure, positive energy that is the Divine ALL.

The good news is that even if you do not believe in the Christ consciousness, evil does.

WHAT IS SPIRITUAL PROTECTION?

A warrior dons armor to protect himself from harm by physical assault. Spiritual protection is like spiritual armor to protect not only one's spirit but also his mind, body and soul. Arrows and bullets afflict only the body, but a spiritual attack can do harm to one's eternal being.

Why do you need spiritual protection?

Everyone needs spiritual protection but most who stay within certain ranges of energy vibration will not require much more than their given sources of protection. In a sense, we all have spiritual protection. It is our birthright as a spirit off-shoot of the Infinite which is pure positive energy. Some call it the light within.

For some, this energy-light is dimmed so much that it is all but obscured from a soul's view. But it is there, eternally. It is also true that nearly every single one of us (with a few exceptions) has been given a guardian or overseer when we came to earth. This spirit may or may not be a family relation but it can be. Other loved ones--friends, family--frequently step in to help you when necessary. You somehow may have a hint of knowing that they are there for you or not sense them around at all. Their purpose is not to be your conscious earth companions anyway.

The average human being having a relatively safe journey will do just fine with these sources of protection. They needn't even consciously be aware of them. They simply follow their gut instincts. Keep from emotional or mental extremes. Maybe pray to a higher power. They're unaffected in any serious way by unauthorized negative influence perhaps due to favorable karmic positioning. (Please keep reading even if you do not believe in karma! Don't throw out the baby with what you might see as the bathwater.)

You who choose to experience more than this, however, will find yourself going into different levels of energy vibration, and usually they will be of a lower frequency. What's the danger in that? Coming up out of that range again can be a formidable task.

Protection from what?

There are a lot of potential problems that can result from not having spiritual protection. Unwanted spiritual contact. Spiritual interference with your mental, emotional, physical and spiritual well-being. Your life--your mind, body and spirit--can be altered most unfavorably from negative energy. You can slip into darkness and not know how to come back. And then there's that little thing about negative spirits and their lovely intentions.

Here are some other potential problems:

- Hauntings. Not only homes but people can be haunted. Spirits can attach to you.

- Relationship problems. Conflicts. Arguments, break-ups. Like attracts like and negativity comes in all forms. Negative energy from spirits will cause upset in your life.

- Physical possession. In some cases, disembodied spirits can take over a person's physical body. They must be invited but people can unwittingly invite them in.

- Curses and hexes. There are some evil-minded people who focus all their negative energy towards others.

- Depression. The misery, darkness and hopelessness one feels when depressed are negative energies.

- Mental problems. Emotional and mental breakdown. Delusions.

- Financial crisis. Abundance is a positive vibration of energy and negativity can drain it away.

- Health problems. Sudden illness and disease. Fatigue. Heart and breathing problems. Physical attacks.

- Falling into eternal darkness. Hell. Being "lost."

Your spiritual strength

Your own eternal spiritual strength is your greatest power that can create and affect more than you know. Your spiritual strength when a conduit for the Eternal Powers that Be is invincible.

People often use the terms "soul" and "spirit" interchangeably but there is a slight yet distinctive nuance of a difference between them. It is easy to see why the confusion because an individual is comprised of *both* soul and spirit, and while on earth, its physical body.

- A spirit is the energy form that is an off-shoot of the ALL, much like a sun ray bursts forth from the sun.

- A soul is an individual consciousness. The mind. (The brain is the physical organ that houses the mind.) Usually, we speak of our spirit when we really mean our soul and spirit together as an identity. Let me try to clarify further:

The soul

A soul is an individual consciousness that was given the gift of being. Being its own individual consciousness apart from the ALL. Why were you given this gift? Because your individual being actually adds to the collective experience, the collective Intelligence, of ALL. I liken this to--and if you're squeamish, please excuse this crude analogy--an animal with infinite number of little projectile-like fingers that are ever-reaching to explore, expand and experience.

A soul can have many incarnations through time, although time is really an illusion here on earth. A soul can accept different earth personas, personalities during different lifetimes. (If you do not believe in such things as reincarnation, you must remain open-minded because on some levels, there is no reincarnation for souls while there it is an offered opportunity or even necessity for others. Hence, religions spout conflicting dogma over this because they misunderstand. Everyone is right; and everyone is wrong.)

A soul's desire or goal is to expand in awareness. (There is more to this but I am trying to simplify to stay on the main topic of spiritual protection.) Souls can elect to merge back into the ALL and forfeit individual identity, and they can re-emerge according to desire.

The spirit

The spirit is one's higher "self" that is, in its purest sense, the same energy that is the ALL. One's spirit is thought of as its own entity but is so only when attached to a soul identity. Spirit exists without a soul, but a soul does not exist without spirit. When you understand these matters, all the religious and spiritual doctrines of the world make sense. What was "mystery" is revealed. The spirit is all-wise. Omnipotent and omniscient. When I speak of one's "spirit" being weak or strong, I refer to the *strength of one's ability to magnify the flow of ALL, the Source of Spirit.*

In the core of your being, your spirit is as the ALL, strong, invincible, infinite. However, while you are in a physical body with an individual soul identity and mind with its own thoughts, you can alter your vibration as to be in disharmony with Spirit. That is like pinching off a water hose. Energy still dribbles out but weakly, weakly.

Weak spirit

What constitutes a weak spirit? Since the Spirit is essentially a higher energy vibration of love, any negative feelings, thoughts or traits that vibrate lower will weaken one's spirit. This pinches your connection with Source of All.

Do you harbor any of the following?

- Fear

- Doubt

- Pride or ego

- Self-loathing

- Hate

- Anger

- Hopelessness

- Depression

- Confusion

- Dishonesty

- Guilt

- Resentment

- Greed

- Domineering or controlling

- Power hungry

Pride and ego are not to be confused with confidence. Self-assuredness comes from knowing of one's own worth in the divine sense. However, when one feels overly prideful of his own self, he cuts himself off from his connection to the Endless Source of All. Then, he will find how small and limited he is on his own.

Strong spirit

On the other hand, it doesn't take much to strengthen one's spirit. Why? Because when humility, honesty, and sincerity are coupled with belief in the

Divine and a little bit of courage, the God-Source-Spirit fills in and gives whatever else is needed. You literally strengthen the connection with pure positive energy. And it *flows*.

Fruits of a strong spirit:

- Courage

- Strong convictions

- Humility

- Honesty

- Sincerity

- Hope

- Good cheer

- Willingness to serve

- Contrition

Contrition is a combination of humility, remorse, and desire to make restitution. It is different from guilt. To have a contrite spirit means to have a conscience and to desire right doing and to have remorse for wrongdoing. This type of remorse actually opens the door to the Divine because one is willing to admit that he, alone, is but a ray of light connected to the Source of Light.

About belief

Belief is a powerful force of energy. Belief powers thoughts and incites action. When proceeding with spiritual exploration, it is vital to be sure about your beliefs. Negative spirits will toy with the weak-minded, especially those with wavering beliefs or unbelief.

Frequently, those who buy haunted homes unawares are those with no or little spiritual beliefs or understanding. Others usually get a sense of the negative energy and walk away. Perhaps, desperation or financial pressure causes people to rush into a haunted house. Sometimes, there are karmic reasons for being drawn towards a particular building.

The specific belief system matters not as long as it is a *positive* one. Spiritual churches who champion evil only channel negative energy. Misuse of even positive church doctrine can elicit negative feelings from their followers (guilt, anger, self-righteousness, condescension, judgment) which actually do more harm than good.

BE SURE YOUR BELIEFS ARE POSITIVE. It's all about energy vibration and positive beliefs are of a high vibration of energy.

How can you tell if your beliefs are positive or negative? How can you tell if a tree is good? What are the "fruits" of your beliefs? What you believe with your heart will "bear fruit" in your outer world. You should see evidence of what it is you believe in your life.

And the fruits of a positive belief system are love, joy, peace, good will to ALL, including your enemies even though, truly, you should have no enemies at all as we all are one. Are you generally optimistic and hopeful?

Believing in God or Christ or a spiritual leader of your choice means nothing without the positive vibrations of love that your belief emanates. Even the devils and demons and all negative spirits "believe" in God. They know He exists. Just *knowing* is not enough because it does not cause you to resonate with the higher energy of love and gratitude. Your beliefs should inspire love, thankfulness and good will to ALL men. Then, you know your beliefs are positive.

No matter what you may choose to believe, I hope you will embrace what I consider to be three sacred truths that transcend every belief system. They will save you from falling into the hands of dark entities and their lies. Hold them in your heart.

THREE SACRED TRUTHS YOU MUST ALWAYS REMEMBER

There are many truths to know but when you come up against negative spirits, there are three sacred truths you must always remember because darkness will confuse you, fill you with doub,t and cause you to forget:

#1. You can never be lost.

To illustrate this concept, I recount an incident involving one of my easily disconcerted aunts who, due to age perhaps, has a very poor sense of direction. She gets "lost" frequently if walking about without an escort. During a family vacation, she went to the restaurant salad bar all by herself as I watched from our table. Preparing to return, she looked around and it was clear she was trying to get her bearings. Casually, her gaze went back and forth to the different sections of the room; then she gulped and panicked. Before I could leap to her aid, she grabbed the arm of a passing server and asked for help. I waved to catch their attention and she was safely delivered back to us.

Was she lost? Everyone knew she was in the restaurant. She knew she was in the restaurant. She couldn't find her way back but I could see her and knew she was never in a bit of danger as I could rush to her side at any given moment. In a spiritual sense, we're all in this same situation. We might feel lost. We might believe we are lost. And belief is a powerful force that can take us to all sorts of places, even into a hell of our own making.

The good news is that Divine Providence always knows right where we are. No matter where we go, our whereabouts are known and there is divine assistance ready to rush to our side if we but ask for it.

So the truth is that we can't really be lost unless we believe we are lost. Sadly, too many souls not only believe they are lost but believe even more strongly that they do not deserve to be found.

#2. You are loved and never alone.

You, your soul, was created out of love. Your spirit is love. Spirit is love. There is no way you cannot be loved. You are worthy of love--no matter what. Never can your spirit be withdrawn from your soul. Your soul can choose to merge into ALL spirit, true, but love is ever-present for you.

You may not feel loved due to other overwhelming feelings at the time. Yet, at the depths of your being, you will *know* that you are loved.

And you're never alone. Again, humans often experience such lowly feelings that seem to obscure the light of truth. Loneliness is an experience but truth be told, your soul never is truly alone. How can it be when we share one spirit? Loneliness is a state of mind. There are too many connected to you, eternally observing you, so the truth is you are never alone.

#3. There is always hope.

Should you fall into negative vibratory places--darkness--you will feel all those negative vibrations that comprise the darkness including grief, sorrow, hopelessness, unworthiness, despair. When you "feel" hopeless, remember the Divine Truth that there is *always* hope. Hope for being restored to light. Hope for all good things. Hope for your highest and dearest desires to come to pass. That is what hope is. It is the light when all seems to have fallen into darkness.

Hope is eternal.

Are there places where hope is forsaken? No. Only where hope is given up by an individual. When one believes there is no hope. Even those who have fallen into the deepest of hells they have created for themselves can be reconciled with the light of love that is God.

But you have to believe there is hope and grab onto it with all of your heart, might, mind, and strength. Hope and more hope shall be added unto you until your light of love will shine brighter and brighter until you find yourself surrounded by light and in the darkness no more.

WHAT IS YOUR ENERGY VIBRATION?

If you want to raise your energy vibration, it isn't that hard to do, depending on your willingness to be humble and see your own shortcomings. You simply need to think, feel and believe positively. This means to embody positive vibrational energies. Love, gratitude, joy, hope, faith, good will. Honesty. Sincerity. Humility.

It is wise to be a good person. Every day, all day. As much as possible. And intention and desire count! We're all human and will err as part of our life experience.

- Forgiveness: This releases so much negative energy within you and others.

- Understanding: If you understood that everyone is doing the best he can with his current level of understanding (Deepak Chopra), you would accept him as he is.

- Tolerance: People have the right to choose their own life experience.

- Patience: Everyone has his or her own timetable of spiritual progression. They might not reach enlightenment this time around. They may have come for different purposes.

- Love: Love for others and not just your own clan is the hallmark of a high vibration.

- Gratitude: Express thankfulness for everything and you're sending out one of the highest vibrations of energy next to love.

- Hope, good will, good cheer: All are high energy vibrations. It is good to make them a part of your spiritual persona.

- Humility and faith: If you are humble enough to ask for Divine help, you will open the doors to Heavenly assistance.

Your armor and weapons

Your energy vibration is your best weapon. If you radiate love and gratitude, you'll have the forces of heaven on your side and dark forces can't touch you because your light dispels darkness.

- Your own positive, loving energy vibration (see previous chapter).

- Love and gratitude. I will show you how to tap them in future chapters.

- Humility. A humble person cannot be manipulated by his ego or pride or vanity which are easy entry points for negativity. (I can't stress this one enough so it is mentioned multiple times in this book.)

- Your positive spiritual beliefs. Positive. Reject the negative beliefs and dogma that bring on guilt, fear, shame, regret, self-righteousness or pride.

- Courage. Evil uses fear against you. Be brave. Be sure.

- Fellowship. Positive souls banding together can be formidable against evil. Friends, family, like-minded community members.

- Knowledge and intelligence. Know thyself. Know thy enemy.

A little knowledge can save you from a lot of bad things.

About talismans, tools and symbols

Such spiritual objects and relics can contain power because they may have been imbued with spirit energy. When spirit energy is infused into an object, the object radiates that positive or negative vibration. Thus, there can be "evil" or "haunted" objects and "blessed" items, too.

Consecrated and Holy items are things that were specifically intended for divine use. Typically, they were prayed over in a religious ritual that dedicated their use for holy purposes which renders them sacred. Holy items were created for religious use. They are tools that the negative spirit will recognize as positive and divine.

Crystals. Planet Earth is a blessed entity for it was set apart to be the physical home for countless souls to experience human life. No one can refute the endless perfectly functioning and intertwined systems that are perfect for sustaining life. Life is divinely appointed. This earth has its own energy vibrations, and earth elements are largely, unless otherwise imbued by humans, positive. Crystals are an example.

Sage. There are many varieties of the sage plant. It is no coincidence that the word "sage" means wisdom and this plant's botanical name is "salvia" which means healing and health. This plant is dried, bundled and burned during ceremonies and its smoke is said to dispel negativity and negative vibrations. It is used chiefly during cleansing and protecting spaces. Native American Indians often used white sage in their spiritual ceremonies.

Salt. As a crystal of earth, salt has been revered pre-dating the time of

Christ. It is mentioned in the bible on numerous occasions with Jesus even drawing an analogy of men to salt ("Ye are the salt of the earth..." Matthew 5:13) Salt has divine energy. It not only is used in rituals of many different religions including Hinduism, Judaism and Shinto, salt has healing and purification quality that staves off bacterial growth and infection. It is said that one can pour a ring of salt around him that evil cannot cross.

Mirrors. Why are mirrors spiritually significant? Mirrors are a symbol of reflection and self-reflection is important for spiritual progression as we strive to evolve. Everyone and everything around us is a mirror, of sorts, reflecting back to us what we choose to see and how we choose to see. Unfortunately for evil spirits, they will see their own misery and darkness. They often lie to themselves and rationalize why they have chosen the dark side but when faced with their own reflection, they see the truth. They see themselves as they are, and they are repelled by it. One can use a mirror to "capture" a negative entity. A prayer for divine assistance and a command to the spirit to "get into the mirror" will force the energy to be trapped into his own reflection. Then, the mirror can be broken which will keep the negative energy in a non-physical dimension. End with a prayer of gratitude.

Symbols. There are many symbols that represent positive energy including love, health and peace. Mandalas represent eternal beauty and change. Amulets are designed with specific intentions for manifesting certain qualities. When symbols are imbued with pure positive energy, they become powerful in their physicality.

Prayers. Prayers are not merely words. They are sincere supplications for Divine aid, verbal expressions of the contents of one's heart, oral and tangible manifestations of one's desires and intentions. They are energy taking form in this physical word. In the bible, it is said, "In the beginning was the Word and the Word was with God, and the Word was God." (John 1:1) Be careful of the words you use in your daily life. Words create because they focus energy. Please use prayer as a powerful call for Divine energy.

A word of caution: It is important to know that unless you wield these with your own power and belief, they can be rendered useless by the opposition.

Items that offer no protection

Divining or dowsing rods, energy monitors, digital recording devices all monitor energy vibrations but offer no protection against negative spirits. Candles and incense may help with clearing energy out of a room but require the focused positive intention of a person. One cannot simply light a candle in a room and expect the candle to do the work by itself.

May I remind you that your strongest tool is your own spiritual energy vibration. Talismans, tools, and symbols merely help focus energy and clarify one's vibrational frequency.

Critical Precautions

You should not go into places with lower energy vibrations if your physical body is weak from illness or poor health. This goes also if you suffer from emotional or mental ailments such as depression, OCD, bipolar disorder or other conditions that affect your beliefs about yourself and life. Your self-esteem should be at a healthy level (too high or too low and you can be easily manipulated). You need to be in good physical, emotional, and spiritual condition or the negative energy will suck the life force out of you too easily.

Paranormal professionals often report not only about the temporary fatigue but the long-lasting effects their type of work has on their psyches. Yet, they consider this a sacrifice in order to offer their gifts. They know how to recharge themselves spiritually and self-protect but even then, every paranormal encounter can leave a little psychic imprint upon you.

Some types of places with lower energy vibrations

- haunted houses

- hostile homes (abuse, chronic anger, criticism and negativity)

- occult gatherings

- dangerous places (violence, crimes, drugs)

- toxic environments (polluted)

- buildings or land with a bad history

- mental institutions and psychiatric wards

- poorly kept nursing homes

- prisons

- cemeteries (some, not all)

- depressing bars or lounges where unhappy people gather

- antique stores

- museums with artifacts with a violent history (not art, botanical, science or children's museums)

- theaters that are showing violent or frightening films

- violent venues (boxing rings, wrestling matches, cock or dog fighting pens)

- casinos (where greed, desperation, want, envy can be rampant)

Any place that brings out negative feelings and thoughts is a place with lower energy vibration. Do not proceed into such a place unless you are prepared and spiritually fortified with only positive intentions, positive beliefs and positive feelings while being on guard for negative changes in any and all.

Mistakes people make when confronting negative spirits

- taunting them (mocking, ridiculing, deriding, laughing)

- challenging them to prove themselves

- making deals with them

- inviting them into one's physical body, mind, life

- getting caught up in the former earth life of the spirit

- feeling sympathy for evil

- believing negative spirits

Remember that everything is about vibration. Negative spirits are vibrating at a very low frequency. Fear is a low vibration. But so are pride and egotism. If you taunt them, you've now lowered your own energy vibration to their level and you become fair game. Without being able to clear your own aura and energy of this negativity, you can become imprinted by negative entities.

I can't stress this enough: Do not play with negative spirits. Some people are called for divine purposes to confront them, but they come with extra spiritual strength and protection that others lack. And everyone and anyone who experiences such, regardless of protection and clearing, will still carry a certain spiritual burden with them for the rest of their earth lives. A risk comes with the responsibility as some negative entities will never forget you and be "gunning" for you. (Again, a strange conception for some to grasp but there is a dimension where this battle between good and evil rages on. You can transcend it, yes, but not when you deliberately engage in the negativity.)

Relief and sympathy are positive feelings, but offered to spirits who are vibrationally low would be like throwing pearls before swine who will trample your good will under their hooves. Negative spirits will warp your good intentions and use them against you. Remember that the evil one is known as the father of all lies. There is no honor or redemption that you can help negative spirits achieve. It must come from a higher source than you. Do not think that you are the one destined to save any soul (this appeals to your ego.) There are ways you can help but never take the word of a negative spirit.

SEVEN SECRETS ABOUT EVIL SPIRITS YOU MUST NEVER FORGET

What is evil?

Some believe that there is no evil. No God. No devil. Truly, I believe that there is so much misunderstanding and confusion over this issue due to everyone's limited definition of God. In our efforts to comprehend something as magnanimous as a "God" entity, we force the infinite and eternal energy of ALL into small man-made concepts. Is He a man? Is He a She? Does He exist at all?

Your understanding of God will continue to evolve as you spiritually progress. There is no need to convince others of your own perception of God because everyone sees God as they need to at the current moment in time. Even those without any religious belief in God can recognize the existence of positive and negative energy. Scientists can identify these energies with physical evidence. There is positive energy and negative energy.

To keep things simple, we define God and goodness with positive energy and positive feelings. Evil is defined as negative energy and negative feelings. So for spiritual protection purposes, there is a God and there is a devil as people collectively have conceived the notions of such. So far now, know thy enemy.

There are many truths to know but when you come up against negative spirits, there are seven secrets you must never forget:

#1. You have power over the negative spirits without a physical body.

The human body is a tremendous gift to us. Your pre-mortal agreement to come to earth to experience life with a human body was both a privilege and an honor. It took great courage to accept this challenge but you did so as a way to spiritually progress and thus add to the collective intelligence of the Divine ALL.

Many positive energy spirits choose not to be born on earth for reasons that will help the collective in other ways. But the negative energy spirits are not able to have a human physical body. They do not have the choice to accept or reject one. (On some cosmic level, they also serve a collective purpose but that knowledge will be divulged at another time.)

When you enter a physical body, you are able to experience this physical earth life and all the highs and lows of human emotions, human creativity and invention and the five physical senses that take in the beauty of life.

Negative vibration spirits without a physical body want one. They want ours. And they try to influence us because they themselves have no power otherwise. If you look at the word "DEVIL" and flip it backwards, you'll see the word "LIVED." A life is sacred. The devil never lived. EVIL is the opposite of LIVE.

There is a difference between a ghost of a person who has died and a spirit who never lived. Ghosts are not evil entities per se. They are the disembodied souls of once living persons, and if their earth personas were evil-minded, their ghosts can stay behind to continue with evil-minded shenanigans but they are not demons or demonic technically speaking.

But just as the light dispels the darkness, positive energy will always send away the negative. You, a positive living soul, have the power of ALL the light that exists and can send away any darkness that attempts to overwhelm you.

#2. They vary in energy strength.

According to some religious beliefs, there are different types of evil demonic entities just as there are different levels of angels. Each have their own areas of dominion and responsibility and thus, varying levels of energy vibration=strength. You can do a study upon this subject, but I will not go into that here. Suffice it to know that you can come across varying levels of demonic strength. You don't need to know about the particular entity's background to send it away. But it may take a more concentrated effort to be rid of those with a stronger energy vibration.

I encourage you to enlist the help of as many like-minded, positive, loving people when you confront a demon because there is strength in numbers. However, you must always remember, too, that you--just one positive and loving soul--have more power than a legion of devils. Take hope and courage in that eternal truth.

#3. They never keep their word.

God keeps His Word. His Word is sacred. God makes promises He never breaks them. The devil? He's at the polar opposite of truth. His word means nothing to him. He never makes or keeps promises. He makes deals and always breaks them. Never enter into a deal with evil. No matter how appealing it may appear. It's all lies.

#4. Fear is their greatest tool against you but it is only an illusion.

When a negative spirit is nearby, people talk about a chill or drop in temperature in the air. You may or may not feel it as some people are less sensitive to temperature. But you will most often sense immediately is uneasiness or dis-ease. "Something" will feel weird, off, strange…just *not right.* Then comes the fear.

You will sense the fear in a room. You will "feel" the fear. But do not own it as your own. The fear you feel is theirs; they fear because they know of their own limited power and influence. But that is all they can use against you by themselves. They can, however, use YOU against yourself.

You can be the source of negativity if you aren't vigilant: doubt, discouragement, pride/vanity, conflict, guilt. Recognize when you are feeling a negative feeling and replace it with love and peace. Negative spirits also can take any human emotion and twist and warp it to make it dark and negative. Even love can become obsessive and motivate people to do bad things in the name of love. Religious wars are fought in the name of God.

There is one emotion that negative spirits cannot emulate: True Peace. Negativity is chaos and unrest. Positivity is true peace.

When in doubt, follow the true peace. You will know it in your heart when you feel it.

#5. They only have power over you if you give it to them.

Your soul already belongs to God. You cannot lose it or offer it in trade. They know this but it won't stop them from trying to get you to allow them to use your physical body and take over your mind. You have the one thing that they want: a physical body in this physical earth plane. They can harass you but not enter you without your permission.

People unknowingly invite them in when they:

- invoke the devil or negative spirits through occult incantations.

- simply address them and enter into conversation with them.

- entertain negative thoughts and engage in negative behavior on a chronic basis.

- choose to enter into a deal or exchange with them.

- get unreasonably angry.

- visit dark places when in a weakened state.

- become ruled by superstition.

- are fearful all the time.

#6. Evil spirits know that they are subject to God and the Christ.

Even if you do not believe in God or Jesus Christ in the conventional, traditional religious sense, evil spirits know of whom we speak. They may mock or deny the power of divinity, but they know they are subject to their command. They, of course, do not want YOU to know that so they will do anything to get you not to believe that God and the Christ consciousness exist.

Although there is more to the Infinite Truth than religion, evil (negative) spirits exist in the dimension where their blessed (positive) opposites exist. Their opposition is the Consciousness that is Love which is the Christ. To combat or protect yourself from evil, you must employ the opposite power which is the Divine.

#7. They must heed what you tell them if you use a key phrase in your command.

Non-religious people, other denominational followers and even spiritual but non-denominational people, misunderstand about the use of the name Jesus Christ. Regardless whether or not you believe in Him in the traditional or conventional sense, as I have previously mentioned, when you are dealing with negative vibrations and negative spirits, they are of the same dimension as their opposite forces which is the positive energy vibration of love which is the Christ consciousnesses. Even if you do not believe this, you will come to find that those self-same negative spirits surely do even if they pretend not to.

All negative spirits are subject to him and they must obey you, too, as a child of God when you use the following phrases:

"In the name of Jesus Christ and the Almighty God, our Heavenly Father…"

"In the name of all that is good and holy which is God, our Eternal Father, the Alpha and the Omega, Dominus Dei..."

One man whose house was being haunted tried his best to command the evil spirit to leave. And the spirit retorted saucily, "And by whose authority do you cast me out?" Unfortunately, the man did not know how to respond and the spirit laughed. The man ended up leaving his house and the negative entity behind to torment the next tenant.

According to the bible, Jesus needed no talisman or holy relic to cast out demons. He simply said, "Get thee hence, satan." And the evil one had to obey. We are blessed to be able to invoke His Name for spiritual protection. Demons must obey His Authority as they are His energy opposite.

The tools of the devil: lies, half-truths and fear

The devil is known as the father of all lies which includes half-lies and half-truths. We are human and all of us have made mistakes for which we are forgiven without you having to do a thing to receive it, except for accept it. Negative spirits will attempt to drag you down into their lower vibrational depths by convincing you of your unworthiness to vibrate any higher.

Do not believe the following:

- You are too sinful to be forgiven.

- You are hopeless.

- God has forsaken you.

- No one loves you.

- You are not worth anything.

- You are going to die.

- You are going to hell.

- Your loved ones will be harmed.

Do you see how all those lies incite fear, hopelessness, doubt, and disbelief in your own worth?

The power of fear

It is natural to sense the fear that will emanate from a negative spirit. It does not mean that you are weak spirited to sense that fear. Courage is the ability to continue through the fear, not letting it stop you from doing what you must do. Fear is like a smoke screen. It is an illusion.

Fire fighters often are asked how they manage to be so brave in the face of a raging fire. How can they charge into burning buildings? They report that once they walk through the smoke, they see where the actual fires are and the fear is gone. It isn't as though they are walking into an all-consuming fire pit as it seems. They see the stairways, the rooms, and where the victims are.

But fear can be a powerful force for those who lack courage. You now must have more courage knowing the sacred truths aforementioned in this book, don't you?

- When feeling fear, take a deep breath. In fact, remembering to breathe in and out during your darkest moments invites the Spirit. The breath of life is holy unto itself.

- Invite the Holy Spirit to dispel fear by offering prayer, talking to God and Christ, singing a spiritual song, feeling love, expressing gratitude and love for God

Danger of superstition

There is a difference between respect for one's beliefs and fear of them. It is always proper to show respect for another's spiritual beliefs. You may not believe in them but they still have some energy to them because others believe in them. Ridiculing them, scoffing at them will open the door to negativity. Remember that ridicule, scorn and scoffing are negative, and like attracts like.

But you need not adopt someone else's beliefs, especially out of fear. A superstition is an irrational belief with fear attached to it.

Do not believe in superstitions. We all can fall victim to superstitions when they are a part of our cultural upbringing. For example, how many of us "knock on wood" when we express a hope for continued good luck? Ever cross your fingers? Sports fans are notorious for their funny superstitious acts. They aren't evil or negative when done in a fun, positive spirit but it is all too easy to allow such matters get out of hand if one becomes obsessive or fearful about them

If you've opened the door to evil

Doors open. Doors can close. It is essential to close a portal that has been open to evil as soon as possible for the more negativity that flows through it, the harder it will be to close it. People ask about portals and doors between dimensions but to explain it will sound like a Hollywood movie. Since my intention for this book is not to explain the workings of the universe but to offer information to protect you spiritually, I will just proceed onward.

People open portals with their intention to allow negative spirits into this earth plane. Why would they do that? Mainly because they are ignorant of the repercussions. Even if they fancy themselves followers of the evil one, they honestly do not know what they are doing. For some reason, while on earth, they have experienced negativity and become filled with more of it. Some are enamored by the "power" of evil. Truly, if they could recall their pre-mortal origins, they would remember that they elected to be born into physical bodies which already indicates which "side" they are on. If truly they were of negative spirit entirely, they would not be here in physical form.

One might point out Hitler or other "anti-Christ" archetypes, but really, they are pawns, albeit notable ones, of the negative side. True evil is…more heinous than can be imagined. Satan followers eventually find their loyalties were grossly misplaced. How can one come back from evil? That is another subject entirely. But take hope: It is not only possible, it is an eventuality for every soul.

How to tell if a portal has been opened

Areas can be haunted by spirits, but the term "open portal" is defined as a space through which disembodied negative spirits can enter this physical dimension. They still do not have flesh bodies but can assume the appearance of physical form. That is why they are often seen as black mists, nebulous energy fields and such but also choose to appear as the most hideous and frightful forms (in an attempt to instill fear). They also can present themselves, temporarily, as a familiar human.

In any case, these types of portals must be opened by someone who intentionally invited negativity and evil into his space. People usually don't have to wonder if a portal has been opened because being anywhere near it will cause a great deal of unease. Other signs can include:

- feelings of foreboding, fear

- anger, conflict, dissention, chaos

- mental confusion

- obscenity

- blasphemy against holy items in the house

- dark dreams and nightmares

- hallucinations

- unearthly or disturbing noises

- paranormal activity (flashing lights, slamming doors, floating objects)

- sickness and serious disease

- sickness and death of animals, pets and plants

How to tell if a negative spirit has attached itself to you

Many people are influenced by negative spirit on a regular basis, unbeknownst to them. Negative spirits love to have some sort of effect upon the living, and they attempt to do so at very opportune moment.

There is a difference between a negative spirit (soul of an ill-intentioned deceased person) and an evil spirit (demon). Generally, if an evil spirit has attached itself to you, you may not be fully aware of it, but those around you will at least suspect it. There will be telltale signs:

- not remembering blocks of time

- being told you said or did things that are not congruous with your normal character

- craving drugs, alcohol, cigarettes or other substances to abuse that you typically have no desire for

- imagining doing violent acts

- feeling uneasy around spiritual or holy places, people and things

- feeling angry without cause

- exhibiting physical symptoms of general un-wellness, dark circles under eyes, sick pallor of skin.

- a "look" in your eyes that is oddly distant or piercingly scary

- not eating at all or suddenly gorging (extremes)

- having no remorse or conscience

- insomnia

- feeling as though "someone" or something is urging you to do things you know are wrong, including committing suicide

If a negative (and not necessarily evil) spirit attaches itself to you, it is said to "follow you around" or even "haunt" you. Look for these signs:

- feeling unusually out-of-sorts, unusual behavior

- out of control

- hallucinations

- becoming obscene

- becoming extremely fearful, sad or angry

- lethargy

- out of the ordinary manic-depressive thoughts

- having "memories" that don't belong to you or your current life

- experiencing terrifying nightmares

- inciting conflict and disturbances in those around you

If you suspect that you are being affected by negative spirits in any way, seek the help of clergy or spiritualists who can assist with your cleansing and protection. Alternatively, you can use the sample protection and cleansing rituals included in this book. However, it is extremely wise to enlist the help of others because your own discernment may be impeded due to the negative interference within you.

How to close a portal

The following explanation is only one ritual that you can use to close a spiritual portal that has been dedicated to allowing negative energy into this physical dimension. There are many but the keys that all should include are here.

If you are of different religious denomination, you may employ the strategies outlined in your religious texts or doctrine as well. However, it has been our experience that the Christ-consciousness appears to supersede polytheistic or New Age beliefs so if you have no success with other religious rituals, please try this. Your belief in God and Christ-consciousness will make it easier for the positive energy to flow forth, yes, but even if you do not believe, remember that the demons do. And that is all that matters. They know of God and Christ. They believe in Them and must obey. However, it will be easier if your belief is connected as the conduit during these rituals so do include people who believe in the circle. Belief is a powerful force.

Ritual helps your focus your attention and intention upon your desire but it is secondary to the energy of your thoughts and intentions.

An example of a ritual to close a portal:

1. Consult local clergy about your situation. Enlist their help. Follow their guidelines. But in the event they either have none or they will not help, continue with the following:

2. Enlist the help of positive, loving, courageous and like-minded friends and family. Avoid including those who are non-believers in spirit matters as they can be vulnerable to negativity. This is not the time to "prove" anything to them nor should them attend just out of curiosity. In the absence of friends, family or clergy, you can find local spiritualists or spiritual organizations who will help or you can proceed alone, if need be.

3. Do not eat, if possible, before any ritual or during any ritual unless the act of eating is a symbolic part of the ritual. If hungry, eat lightly prior to the ritual performance. Fasting, if you can do it, is best. But if you can't fast without becoming famished, your body will only feel weak.

4. Be clear about your positive intention. State it aloud and be sure all in attendance can do the same.

5. Stand in a circle around or near where you believe the portal has been opened. Join hands. This represents eternity and the eternal bond of love and friendship that will strengthen all those present. You may choose to encircle your circle with a ring of natural sea salt or crystals.

6. Breathe in deeply and slowly several times, and be sure all in attendance do the same as everyone recognizes the divinity of the Breath of Life. Life is sacred. Negative spirits do not have a physical body that can breathe or take in LIFE.

7. Prayer. Begin with a prayer (See the Index of Prayers).

8. State the verbal command (See the Index of Prayers.)

9. You may choose to wear any Holy symbols that you feel with protect

you. You may choose to use Holy water, consecrated oil or the Holy Cross during your prayer.

10. After the negativity is gone, you should feel a lightness and a peace in the area. People often report a feeling of fresh air. This is when you should immediately rededicate this area for only good purposes.

11. Always, always end any ritual with a prayer of gratitude. Let this flow from your heart.

After the closing of a portal:

1. Light. Fill the area with natural sunlight.

2. Fresh air. Open up windows and doors to let in fresh air.

3. Cleanse the room/area with fresh, clean water if possible.

3. Sacred music. Play uplifting, joyful music in the area. Sing!

4. Nature. Invite nature in with real plants, flowers, animals, children, friends. Socialize here in a most happy way.

5. Remember what happened here no more. Don't retell the story of this open portal as negative spirits would like nothing more than to be kept alive (live) in your memory and in this space.

6. Keep this area clean from filth. Decorate pleasantly with positive symbols.

7. Rededicate this area with a declaration and prayer of good intention ("We dedicate and consecrate this area in the name of God as holy ground for only the highest good for all who enter" or something similar.) Continue to inhabit this space with love and gratitude.

How to cleanse your environment

Cleansing your environment is similar to closing a portal, except that the prayer is different because the intention is different. Please use the prayer included in the Index of Prayers as only a guideline. It is best for you to pray in words that spring forth from your heart, spontaneously and sincerely.

Do include clergy who can not only cleanse your environment of negativity but then dedicate your home or space to divinity and the higher good for all.

How to cleanse yourself

Consider your own physical body as the dwelling for your spirit. It is its own building, is it not? Baptisms symbolize a cleansing and dedication to belief in the Christ. Non-Christian religions have their forms of cleansing of the body, mind, and spirit, too, often using water ablutions.

As with the previous rituals, this one is just an example of what one could do to symbolically cleanse oneself. However, if you feel that you may have become possessed or are being haunted by evil spirit, it is very important to find clergy or spiritualist who can help you.

However, as a precaution, you can proceed as follows:

1. Find clergy or spiritualists who will conduct a cleansing ritual for you.

2. Enlist the help of like-minded, positive and loving friends and family.

3. Be clear about your intentions and state them aloud.

4. Ask everyone in attendance to create a circle around you and join hands.

5. Draw a circle of natural sea salt around their circle.

6. Begin with prayer. (See Index of Prayers for examples, but it a self-cleansing, it is good to speak spontaneously.) Express gratitude and ask for forgiveness. Express your desires for being cleansed.) Ask everyone to please forgive you and to send you loving thoughts during this process.

7. Envision a pillar of white light coming down upon you, purifying your body. You may use symbols here like pouring Holy water upon you or using a few drops of consecrated oil on your head. Although it is not necessary, you can also change your clothes to new or clean clothing to symbolize taking on a new self.

8. Re-dedicate yourself to serving on the highest good for all.

9. End with a prayer of gratitude.

After a cleansing:

It is important to be clean in mind, body, and spirit after a spiritual cleansing.

1. Avoid slovenliness.

2. Consider the symbolism of what you wear. Wear what you stand for.

3. Keep clean thoughts.

4. Utter only clean words.

5. Do only clean deeds or actions.

6. Listen to positive, uplifting music and films.

7. Read positive, uplifting books and articles.

8. Keep clean company.

Where to turn for help

If you should meet unsavory and dangerous spirits, it is better if you have help on your side.

- Clergy. Keep contacting clergy until you find one who can and will help. Many are unequipped to deal with the supernatural due to their own weak spirits or lack of understanding. This varies by individual, not by church.

- Specific cultural spiritual healers. If the origins or background of a spirit are known, it is good to find a spiritual contact of the same background. Native American Indian souls will feel more trusting towards a spiritual healer who is of their same tribe, for example.

- Psychic mediums. There is an old saying in the psychic field that "all mediums are psychic but not all psychics are mediums" which means that there are different modalities of psychic perception and being able to communicate or perceive spirits is only one type. Find a medium who can communicate with spirits for they will be able to provide a lot of information about the spirit you're dealing with.

- Paranormal investigators. Skilled paranormal investigators have experienced negative spirits before and they often have reliable resources for willing clergy, healers, mediums and such to share with you.

- Spiritually-minded friends. There is strength in numbers of peaceful, loving, faithful human beings.

- Jesus Christ. There is a Christ-consciousness that is a loving vibration whether or not you are a follower of any religion.

- God Himself. Ask of Him and He will sent legions of angels to aid you.

About God, Christ and angels

You might have very different spiritual beliefs as far as God, Jesus Christ, and heavenly angels. Perhaps, you are a Buddhist or Muslim or Wiccan or Pagan. When I use the terms "God" "Jesus Christ" and "angels" I know that they bring up specific images in most minds, but theirs is a reality that transcends what man's religions have defined for the masses. I do not speak of the God, the Christ, and angels that are so depicted in the limited, narrow scope of man-made texts.

Someday, you will learn how all religions are reaching for the same God but offer people what they need to know at their current level of understanding, much like stepping stones to a higher place. All are wrong; yet all are right. It has been man's greatest folly to fight against one another in the name of God. With the diversity of races, there needs to have been a diversity of expressions of God and our love for Him.

No matter which religious doctrine you adhere to or if you adhere to none at all, know this: If there are evil spirits (and the devil), there must be good spirits and God. Even if you believe that Jesus is a myth, at least recognize the energy and consciousness of that myth.

There is a realm or dimension where the Christ-consciousness reigns. It is a powerful consciousness, an all loving spirit. It is this eternal spirit you can call upon for help because He is of the highest energy vibration that will obliterate anything negative which, in biblical terms, means that He has dominion over evil.

Even non-Christians have witnessed demonic spirits mention the Christ by name and loathe to have to depart under His command. One needn't be a church-goer to call upon the Christ. Even if previously you did not "believe" in Jesus Christ, you may use His name to dispel negative spirits because *they* believe in Him. They know of His vibrational power, of His divinity. Light casteth out all darkness (evil).

Whatever is the ultimate reality of realities, the ALL, it will help you to accept that while in *this* dimension dealing with *these types* of negative spirits, they are subject to Him. It may or may not be that way in other dimensions but we shall learn more about that another time.

PROTECTION FOR SPECIFIC SITUATIONS

Protection for a home

Protection for a home is similar to a cleansing but just proactively so. You'll still want to "banish" negativity and negative spirits from your home in case there were stowaways or lurkers that you were unaware of. They can hitchhike on visitors or workers who enter your abode as one did when we had some construction done on our house. It was the father of one of the workers who took a liking to me and hid in the closet. Gone now but unsettling at the time.

1. Clean the home. Use fresh, clean water. As you clean, feel gratitude.

2. Air it out with plenty of fresh air through open windows, if possible.

3. If you feel better using symbols, you can dedicate some sea salt and pour it all around the perimeter of your entire property, being careful not to sprinkle it on grass or living plants, only cement structures. On grassy areas, use Holy Water or water that has been purified and blessed by you through prayer (See A prayer to bless and purify water.) Put up any symbols or talismans that you believe in.

4. Say a prayer of protection (See A prayer to protect a home.) Conduct a cleansing and send any entities out (See A prayer to cleanse a home and to send a ghost into the light.)

5. Keep the home filled with good feelings, especially love, joy, peace and good will. Clean laughter is good, too.

6. Keep negative items, including negative books, movies and music, out of your house. Negative means anything that invites a dark or foreboding feeling. Violence, anger, depression. Physical and spiritual filth are lower vibrations.

7. Express love and gratitude often while in your home for your home and for all who enter into it and especially for God. Use your home for positive purposes (to be a peaceful, happy refuge, a healing oasis for visitors, a loving gathering spot.) It is nice to dedicate your home for good purposes.

Apartments

Apartments can harbor negative spirits either in one apartment or the entire apartment building. The collective energy of all the tenants matters. Are your neighbors generally happy and honest?

You can protect your apartment in the same way you do for a house but say prayers for the entire apartment building and its tenants.

Protection while traveling

The spirit world is here with us, just a few strings of dimensions away. Everywhere we go, spirits may roam. Thankfully, we do not see them all or it would be extremely disconcerting and difficult to focus on our own lives here. (Select people don't have this privilege as their roles are different than ours. God bless them for the sacrifices they must make in order to help spirit-souls.)

When you travel, don't dwell upon the negative. Fearful attention attracts negative spirits. And do your best to stay away from places known for their negativity (violent or dark history, etc.) If you must, do what you feel will give you peace and freedom from fear. Prayer, ritual. But rituals are only for your own focus and peace of mind.

Remember that your own positive energy vibration is your best armor against negative spirits. Like attracts like. You won't sense ghosts and negative spirits so easily because they are at a lower vibration and you will gravitate towards higher vibrational places and beings.

1. Say a prayer to dedicate your travel to God and the highest good for all.

2. Ask for divine protection.

3. Keep your vibration high.

4. Wear or bring any talismans that you believe in.

5. Meditate and envision a circle of white light of sacred protection around you.

6. Sprinkle consecrated sea salt around your sleeping abode.

7. Air out the hotel room you are in with a cleansing prayer. Don't light candles for they can be used against you and start a fire.

8. Fill your hotel room with light, uplifting music, fresh air and positive feelings (prayer, laughter, good thoughts).

Protection while ghost hunting

Ghost hunting seems to be popular today even for those who are looking to be convinced that the paranormal exists. They fancy a night of being spooked not realizing the potential dangers that lurk. It is not uncommon for even a seasoned ghost hunter to become affected by negative spirits. Not just physically attacked but spiritually influenced. The negativity can change a personality, destroy relationships, sicken people and ruin finances. They can become prideful, angry, argumentative. Sometimes, the persons involved don't even recognize it is happening.

Some of those television personalities who hunt for ghosts are seen taunting the ghosts into showing some visual reaction for their cameras. Since ghosts are usually benign, deceased people, they may or may not comply with a flash of lights or even a voice recording. But mock and taunt the wrong type of spirit, the negative spirit, and they can unleash a lot of negative energy. Ghost hunters have been clawed at and sickened on camera but what the producers do not show the viewers is the negative effects that linger on after the director says, "Cut!" Did you know that one man contracted a serious even terminal illness? Others severed social ties with each other.

Usually, the ghost investigator has his/her resources to turn to in the event of negative spiritual attachment but for you, it is wise to protect yourself before you head out for your ghost adventures.

A few minutes of quiet, prayerful meditation can be highly effective. Set your intentions in your mind or aloud. What are you trying to achieve? Be sure you have only positive intentions for everyone involved including the spirits who you may meet. Don whatever holy symbols that hold meaning for you. Ask for protection in the name of Christ and God.

If any negative thoughts or feelings arise within you, redirect them back to a positive place. Do not entertain any negative thoughts even if you begin to believe they are sound and reasonable.

1. Say a prayer to dedicate the ghost hunt to God and ask for protection.

2. Keep your vibration high.

3. Wear or bring any talismans that you believe in. It is good to bring Holy water, Holy cross and consecrated sea salt with you. You may or may not believe in such but the negative spirits can feel the positive and divine

energy attached to these sacred items and have an aversion to them, much like opposite magnetic fields.

Protection during spiritual-occult practices

First, let's clarify the definition of the word "occult" because there's a lot of misunderstanding. Occult by biblical definition is evil but many people today must lump their interests into that umbrella term when their activities are far from evil. Divination tools, such as the tarot, astrology, runes, Iching, are subject to the intentions of their users. Many people use these tools to aid others in very positive ways.

However, some tools (the Ouiji Board is a good example) were created with negative intentions. I highly entreat everyone to stay away from these types of negative devices.

I also strongly implore you to stay away from any divining tools of any sort if you intend to use them for negative purposes and with negative energy. Voodoo dolls, hexes, hate potions or even love potions that rob someone of free will are all items that will intensify the negativity and redirect it back to the user (you) with effects that can span lifetimes.

If you choose to use these items, protect yourself from negativity with positive intentions, prayers and any rituals that will reconfirm your dedication to the highest good for all. Cleanse and dedicate your tools in the same way. Use sunlight, blessed water, sage, salt, crystals to bless your tools. Everything brought forth by these tools should be to bless the lives of others and not harm anyone.

1. Cleanse yourself and your environment.

2. Cleanse your spiritual tools. There are many symbolic ways to accomplish this with sunlight, the moon in various phases, with blessed water, but in actuality, these are the rituals that are meant to focus all of YOUR energy and positive intention that will help conduct the flow of pure, positive universal energy. That energy is what is being imbued into your tools. All the energy from the sun, moon, earth elements and water certainly cannot hurt and they can and do magnify cosmic energy but it is nothing compared to your own energy. "Is it not written in your law and I said ye are gods?" (John 10:43) If you truly understood the power of human spirit, you would know that in our own way, we are as the stars in cosmos, emitting waves of energy with our own fission.

3. Dedicate your tools and your work with them to the highest good for all. Use them with love and gratitude.

Protection during exorcism

An exorcism is a ritual performed to rid a human being of a negative spirit that has entered into his physical body. Can you conduct an exorcism alone? Yes. Should you? Probably not. There is spiritual strength in numbers.

Also, negative spirits vary in their own strength. A ghost is the spirit-soul of a deceased person who has not crossed over upon death. A spirit-soul may choose to stay behind for any number of reasons but occasionally due to the death circumstance, the individual may be "lost" in the spirit dimension. Usually, he is simply confused and stays close to what is familiar to him, his earth home. Some ghosts are quite harmless to us while others can be just as mean and nasty as they were as living people. We can refer to some of these ghosts as negative spirits because they are so darned malevolent and of a negative vibration but truly negative spirits are different.

A negative spirit, on the other hand, a spirit identity that never had a physical body. It is a negative vibration of energy. It does have its own identity, just not a body. Do they have their own souls? Truthfully, I do not know. This has not yet been revealed to me. In some religious traditions, they do indeed have their own souls but they are condemned and lost. That does not ring true to me in my own sense of cognizance. In some higher realm, I do believe that we will come to find that they are all puffs of smoke, illusions that served a purpose for collective growth and understanding. Perhaps, that is why during direct communication with some negative spirits, they offer their names like "legion" or "fear" with very few giving an individual name. Some do, but who can believe evil?

An exorcism is a religious ritual so it is best to leave it to the religious clergy experienced in these matters. A person requiring the exorcism will be given spiritual protection during the actual procedure with prayer. You will be instructed by them as to the best way for you to be protected during an exorcism, as an observer I'd presume, but remember to ask for protection during your own prayers before, during and after the sessions. Do your best to maintain a trusting, faithful, humble, loving, hopeful, peaceful energy within you before, during and after the exorcism.

Protection of children

Blessed are the children for they come with extra protection and you can see this by their pure spirits and high energy vibrations. But they can be vulnerable to negativity and negative spirits, too.

If my home were plagued by a negative spirit, I would remove my family from it immediately on a temporary basis until the house was cleansed and the spirit was expelled. Some people have nowhere to go, I understand, and in that case, I would continue to make the house cleansing a priority while protecting my children.

- Keep your children by you at all times.

- Pray for them and ask for God's protection.

- Invoke the help of any of your spiritual ancestors who love and care about the child.

- Fill the house with love, light, fresh air and live plants.

- Encircle the place where you and your children sleep with salt.

- Ask the local clergy to bless them with a special prayer of protection.

- Take your children out in nature to renew their energy. Safe parks, for example.

- Express love and gratitude to them and for them throughout the day.

- Refrain from getting angry at them for any reason.

- Command the negative spirits to leave your children alone in the name of all that is good and holy even Jesus Christ and the Almighty God of this Universe.

- Overlook any negative behavior or attitudes that your children might exhibit during this time. It is not their true selves but the expression of the negativity they are sensing.

Protection of pets

Animals perceive energy even more readily than we do because their natural physical bodies are biologically designed to sense higher and lower energy frequencies than our human organs can. You've heard of dog whistles and

high pitched sounds that our "out of human range" of hearing, right? They can sense spirit presence.

Animals are especially vulnerable to negative spirits not just because they can sense them but they have little defense against them. While animals exude positive energy, they also absorb readily the energies in their environment. They will become fearful, agitated and even violent in the presence of negative spirits. Pets have been known to absorb so much negativity and experience so much stress from this that they perish.

If it were me, I would remove my pets from the premises until the negative situation gets reversed. If you cannot do that, be sure to take your pets out for walks in nature as much as possible to renew their energy. Ask for blessings for your pets from local clergy. Pray for them yourself.

Keep them near you as much as possible. Encircle their beds with salt. Command the negative spirits to leave your pets alone in the name of Jesus Christ who loves all the beasts and creatures of this earth. Ask for divine assistance from all who love animals. There are legions who do.

Protection during dream state

We all have a certain vulnerability during our dream state. If there are negative spirits in the place where you sleep, you most likely will dream about them. The dream dimension is a dimension of spirit, and negative spirits as well as the positive spirits can be perceived here.

Years ago, I met a dark and haunted woman. Her real eyes were covered by these artificially blue contact lenses and they looked inhuman really. She admitted to me that she had entered into a "deal" with the devil himself in order to be granted her visa to the Unites States and to be promised that a newborn family member would be left alone by evil. Remember that evil always makes deals and never keeps them, but for her, it was too late to prevent her from entering into this most unfortunate exchange with the dark side. She told me that the moment she cried out to the devil, someone knocked on her door in the middle of the night offering her an envelope that contained her visa. Now this all sounds like stuff straight out of a Hollywood horror flick but I assure you, this was real life.

Ever since then, she said, she was haunted by the sounds of marching soldiers and shadow figures following her to be sure she kept her end of the bargain. I did not ask what she promised but she volunteered that she "would do whatever" they (demons) asked. Ominously, she said she "did something for them" once and they wanted her to do it again: And then she looked at me and I knew she wanted to kill me.

Instantly, I prayed and saw a white light of protection come down. The Hand of God extended to me as I heard: "Is this what you want? She is only on the periphery of evil." I told Him what I wanted and that was to stay within the light of goodness. This woman looked about me, curiously, and I knew that she could see this, too. A sudden knock on the door startled us both and it was my son coming to my rescue to whisk me out of there. But later that night and for several nights afterward, this woman's personage appeared to stand over me with her haunting artificial blue eyes. "Please help me," she beseeched. My compassion for her confused me and I had to turn to clergy for help. I was advised not to allow evil to use my compassion against me lest I be drawn into her same sorrowful state. I was assured that if she was sincere about wanting to turn from evil, help for her would come from another source and not me. After prayer, cleansing and protection, the nightmares stopped and I forgot all about her.

It will be difficult to prevent spirits from entering your dreams until you get rid of them during your wakeful state. Attend to that expulsion of negative spirits by cleansing your home and every room in your house. Cleanse yourself. Say prayers before bedtime.

Occasionally, a spirit will attach itself to the person and not the house itself. When this happens, it is good to approach this situation like a possession and get an exorcism or priest blessing. At the very least, perform a cleansing of yourself. If the situation persists, you might contact a spiritual medium who can provide any karmic details to see if there is unfinished business between you and the spirit who is following you around and what can be done about it. Be sure to own your own power and command the spirit to leave you in the name of Christ and God then be sure to surround yourself with positive energy and love.

Some will fill their bedrooms with sacred symbols, even encircling their beds with salt. Whatever helps you feel safe and protected will release you from fear. And that is a good thing.

About your physical body

Your physical body is a gift beyond measure. Scientists are learning how stunningly complex the human body systems are and wonder how the body has evolved to the degree that allows it to reproduce, grow, heal and think. It is a magnificent vessel for our soul-spirit to experience human life like no other life form can.

Without our physical body, we cannot exist here in this physical dimension so our bodies are not to be disregarded or treated with anything less than loving reverence. Alas, our human impulses and senses yearn for more experiences--all types of experiences--and that can lead to overindulgence, self-harm and disrespect.

I encourage you to treat your body like the temple of spirit it is. That does not mean to say you must restrict and limit your life experiences. Just choose which ones you would like to experience and if it so harms your body, accept the physical consequences as part of the irrevocable physical laws of this universe. Cause and effect.

With that said, there spiritual forces at work supersede the physical. That is why Jesus said, "There is nothing from without a man, that entering into him can defile him: but the things which come out of him, those are they that defile the man." (Mark 7:15) But He meant spiritual defilement. The physical body can still perish with mistreatment.

People ask me if what they eat is important for spirituality. That is an entirely different subject with many important thoughts but for the purposes of this ebook and its goal of spiritual protection, let us keep it simple:

Eat and drink with **gratitude**. It is true that there are some plants and foods that have higher energy vibrations but the effect is always about how your personal body is *affected;* and with prayer and positive intention, your body can raise its energy vibration no matter what you eat. This is not permission to overindulge and consume known toxins. But there is no need to fret over the symbolism of every single morsel that enters your mouth. It can't hurt if the intentions are good but do not allow your thoughts to become too rigid and/or fearful about what you eat because both are negative energy thoughts.

With that said, it is better not to eat before going ghost hunting or performing any spiritual ritual. A full stomach puts physical demands on the body systems which would be better on full alert during spiritual or paranormal activity. If you're famished, that is not a good or positive state so eat. But eat lightly.

If you are familiar with fasting as religious ritual, fasting can be a powerful way to focus your spiritual energy. If not, fasting can be just a drain on your appetite and will power, negative vibrations.

THE ULTIMATE BATTLEGROUND: YOUR HEART AND MIND

Earthly wars are fought on bloody battlegrounds but spiritual wars are fought in the realm of spirit. Misguided souls may believe that their man-against-man efforts are motivated by a spiritual cause, but truth be told, the only true spiritual fight is man against himself. Outsiders may assail you but the way to resist or overcome is to rise up in spiritual-energy vibration. Rise above the negativity.

That takes place in one's heart and mind. Keep both clean and positive to magnify your inner light so that darkness cannot exist where you stand.

Continually reflect on your thoughts, words and behavior. Be honest and sincere at all times. Be filled with love, peace, forgiveness and tolerance. Yes, those are the most effective weapons in your spiritual arsenal. This book on spiritual protection does not get into the battle within. That is another book entirely. But protect yourself by bolstering your heart and mind with good thoughts. Always. Especially about your own self. Darkness will use you to attack yourself through self-doubt, depression and low self worth. Never belief the lies about yourself. Know you are of infinite value.

And always, always be sure you know without a doubt which side you are on. This is not a matter of your self-worth so do not judge yourself here. Simply choose. Choose which side you desire to be on. And choose wisely for this choice has far-reaching soul implications.

May you be blessed with spiritual protection on your journey, my soul friend. And I thank you for your sincere intentions and efforts to do good. Live well. Fare well. Let your light shine on.

INDEX OF PRAYERS

Do not let the word 'prayer' put you off if you are not religious. A prayer is a powerful statement of intention and thus energy. A prayer can start a flow of energy, positive or negative. I use the word 'prayer' for lack of better word.

Prayer does, however, insinuate the belief in something that one is praying to. If not your God, you at the very least invoke the cosmic power of positive energy that you need to deal with the negative energy you encounter.

Remember when I said that hope and humility are critical? You may not have figured out the mysteries of God but until then have hope that it all makes sense and it is all true and have the humility to pray to a higher positive power. You are a million watt light bulb with the entire cosmic electric generator to power you up if you but flip a switch through humble prayer.

Many an atheist has "found God" after a run-in with the dark side.

About mentioning specific names

When praying for specific individuals, it is good to state their full, given names. If it is unknown, that is all right as well since they are known by their Creator and the divine energy from which they sprung.

Some who perform exorcisms or banishments/cleansings like to know the name of the negative entity or evil demon they are expelling. By the command in the name of God and the Christ, demons must give their names to you. However, it is entirely unnecessary to ask. It only tempts you to engage in conversation with evil and evil can be cunning in twisting your words and thoughts until you are confused and vulnerable. Better just to get on with the exorcism using all-encompassing names for them such as "you who inhabit this body and invade this home and all of your evil embodiments" or "every evil entity who is here" or "God in heaven, please banish all of the evil entities and negative energies…" "YOU know who you are. I address YOU and command YOU to get out!"

Here are examples of prayers that I use but words need not be memorized and used verbatim. It is your energy and intention in your words that hold power. In the bible, Jesus said to "pray in this manner" when He said what is now known as "The Lord's Prayer" and now everyone recites it word for word. They truly are empty words without one's *loving and sincere feelings.* Please imbue all of your prayers with sincere gratitude and love.

You can say whatever you wish so long as the "spirit" of these prayers are included in what you say. There is one exception: You must mention the Almighty God and Christ in your words. They transcend religious denomination in the spirit world.

It is good to pray throughout your daily life simply by expressing your love and gratitude for everyone and everything. "When you do this to the least of them, you have done it unto me," Jesus said.

A prayer and command to cleanse a home

"Dear Heavenly Father, our loving Creator, the Source of all that is good and holy,

I thank you with all of my love for the blessing of this house and home. I am grateful to be given a safe and secure home to live in. It appears to have been intruded upon by negative spirits and I need Thy divine help.

Please protect this home from negativity and negative spirits. Please send them from whence they came, even the outer darkness. Please protect us from harm by their negativity.

Please cleanse this home so all who enter will be safe and at peace. I dedicate this home to You and the higher good of all.

In the name of the Christ and all that is good and holy. Amen."

Then, directly aloud:

"I command you and all the negative spirits who have entered this home to LEAVE NOW AND GO BACK TO THE OUTER DARKNESS, in the name of Jesus Christ and the Almighty God of the Universe, the Alpha and the Omega, Dominus Dei, the Divine Master."

Repeat the command. You do not need to repeat the prayer as it will have been imprinted upon the positive flow of energy but negative spirit can resist so do repeat the command often with courage and conviction and belief. Occasionally, the strength or number of entities will require stronger and more focused energy that you might be able to muster by yourself but if you believe, you can do this alone with Divine aid. Sometimes, it becomes a matter of "the party here is over for you. You don't have to go home but you can't stay here." They may not go back to outer darkness but they will have to leave your presence and abode. I do not like to use this tactic often as they will go off to pester other people in other places.

If you hear conversation and challenges from negative spirit, do not reply. Simply repeat the command over and over.

A prayer to cleanse yourself

"Dear Heavenly Father, our loving Creator, the Source of all that is good and holy,

I thank you with all of my love for the blessing of my being and for my physical body. I am grateful to be given a physical body through which I learn so much about life. I am thankful to experience human life!

My physical body appears to have been intruded upon by negative spirits and I need Thy divine help.

Please protect my physical body and my mind and soul from negativity and negative spirits. Please send these evil spirits from whence they came, even the outer darkness. Please protect me from harm by their negativity.

Please cleanse my physical body, mind and soul so I may be free from evil and be both safe and at peace. I dedicate myself, my physical body, mind and soul to You and the higher good of all.

In the name of the Christ and all that is good and holy. Amen."

Then, directly aloud:

"I command you and all the negative spirits who have entered me to LEAVE NOW AND GO BACK TO THE OUTER DARKNESS, in the name of Jesus Christ and the Almighty God of the Universe, the Alpha and the Omega, Dominus Dei, the Divine Master."

Repeat the command. You do not need to repeat the prayer as it will have been imprinted upon the positive flow of energy but negative spirit can resist so do repeat the command often with courage and conviction and belief.

If you hear conversation and challenges from negative spirit, do not reply. Simply repeat the command over and over.

A prayer to close a portal

"Dear Heavenly Father, our loving Creator, the Source of all that is good and holy,

I thank you with all of my love for the blessing of You and all the legions of divine angels and positive beings. I am thankful for the knowledge You have given us regarding protecting ourselves from evil.

It appears that someone has opened a portal to allow negative spirits to enter this physical dimensions and I need Thy divine help.

Please close this portal to protect people here on earth. Please send back all the evil spirits who have come through it and shut this door so evil may enter no more to cause harm to Your beloved children on earth!

We love you and we may make mistakes but we know You love us and will protect us from our own follies. Please close this portal and purify this site so we may dedicate it to You and all that is good and holy, that it may bring love and peace instead of ill.

In the name of the Christ and all that is good and holy. Amen."

Then, directly aloud:

"I command you and all the negative spirits who have entered through this portal to RETURN AND GO BACK THROUGHT THIS DOOR AND INTO THE OUTER DARKNESS, in the name of Jesus Christ and the Almighty God of the Universe, the Alpha and the Omega, Dominus Dei, the Divine Master."

Repeat the command. You do not need to repeat the prayer as it will have been imprinted upon the positive flow of energy but negative spirit can resist so do repeat the command often with courage and conviction and belief.

If you hear conversation and challenges from negative spirit, do not reply. Simply repeat the command over and over.

A prayer to protect children

"Dear Heavenly Father, our loving Creator, the Source of all that is good and holy,

I thank you with all of my love for the blessing of children [name them by name if praying for specific children]. They bring such love and joy to all they meet. I love them with all of my being and I know You do, too.

Please protect these children and all children on earth from the negativity that can assail us all. Please protect them from harm from both earthly and unearthly energies. Keep them safe and happy and loved. Encircle them with Your divine power, protection and love. Please send them legions of holy angels to protect them when needed.

I pledge to do my best and whatever is within my power to protect them and raise them to know and love You and serve only the highest good.

Please protect them from evil at all times.

In the name of the Christ and all that is good and holy. Amen."

Then, directly aloud:

"I command you and all the negative spirits to LEAVE THESE CHILDREN ALONE AND GO BACK TO THE OUTER DARKNESS, in the name of Jesus Christ and the Almighty God of the Universe, the Alpha and the Omega, Dominus Dei, the Divine Master."

Repeat the command. You do not need to repeat the prayer as it will have been imprinted upon the positive flow of energy but negative spirit can resist so do repeat the command often with courage and conviction and belief.

If you hear conversation and challenges from negative spirit, do not reply. Simply repeat the command over and over.

A prayer to protect animals or pets

"Dear Heavenly Father, our loving Creator, the Source of all that is good and holy,

I thank you with all of my love for the blessing of these precious and beautiful animals whom You love, too.

Please protect them from harm by evil and negative spirits. Please encircle them with Your love and protection so negativity cannot enter their vulnerable minds and bodies. They are so special, oh God. They protect me physically but I need Thy help to protect them spiritually.

In the name of the Christ and all that is good and holy. Amen."

Then, directly aloud:

"I command you and all the negative spirits LEAVE THESE ANIMALS AND PETS IN MY HOME AND PROPERTY ALONE AND GO BACK TO THE OUTER DARKNESS, in the name of Jesus Christ and the Almighty God of the Universe, the Alpha and the Omega, Dominus Dei, the Divine Master."

Repeat the command. You do not need to repeat the prayer as it will have been imprinted upon the positive flow of energy but negative spirit can resist so do repeat the command often with courage and conviction and belief.

If you hear conversation and challenges from negative spirit, do not reply. Simply repeat the command over and over.

A prayer to bless and purify water

"Dear Heavenly Father, our loving Creator, the Source of all that is good and holy,

I thank you with all of my love for the blessing of water. Pure, clean water is life to us here on earth, and I am grateful for every drop. You are the living waters.

Please bless and purify this water {in this glass, in this bottle, in this well, etc.] to restore it to its natural and God-given state. May every particle be re-energized with pure positive energy and love, cleanliness and life!

I dedicate this water to You and all that is good and holy. May it be used with great love and appreciation and for the highest good. Please bless this water to make it holy and powerful for all good and against all evil. May this water be as Living Waters of the Christ.

In the name of the Christ and all that is good and holy. Amen."

Then, directly aloud:

"Water, God has blessed you to be restored to your natural and God-given purity and power. You are a representative of the Living Waters of Christ and dedicated for only holy and positive purposes for the highest good. We love you and thank you.

In the name of Jesus Christ and the Almighty God of the Universe, the Alpha and the Omega, Dominus Dei, the Divine Master."

Once is sufficient.

However, I caution you that once water has been blessed in this manner, it is vital to treat it with great reverence and care. Dis-respect by you will render the water powerless, lifeless and will incur negative repercussions for you.

A prayer to consecrate objects

Consecrate objects with similar intention and words as above.

"Dear Heavenly Father, our loving Creator, the Source of all that is good and holy,

I thank you with all of my love for the blessing of this [name of object.] I appreciate this because [state why you are thankful for it.]

I dedicate this [object] to You and all that is good and holy. May it be used with great love and appreciation and for the highest good. Please bless this [object] to make it holy and powerful for all good and against all evil.

In the name of the Christ and all that is good and holy. Amen."

Then, directly aloud:

"[Object], God has blessed you to be imbued with pure positive energy and divine power. You will stand for and serve only holy and positive purposes for the highest good. We love you and thank you.

In the name of Jesus Christ and the Almighty God of the Universe, the Alpha and the Omega, Dominus Dei, the Divine Master."

Once is sufficient.

Again, I strongly implore you to treat any blessed or consecrated object with great reverence and care. Dis-respect by you will render the object powerless, lifeless and will incur negative repercussions for you.

A prayer while traveling

"Dear Heavenly Father, our loving Creator, the Source of all that is good and holy,

I thank you with all of my love for the blessing of being able to travel throughout this beautiful Earth.

As I do so, please protect me and all of my fellow travelers from harm by evil and negative spirits. Please encircle us with Your love and protection so negativity cannot harm, influence or affect us

As we travel, may we spread love, joy and good will everywhere we go and lend a hand when possible.

In the name of the Christ and all that is good and holy. Amen."

You may wish to say a protection prayer for your temporary abodes before you enter and before you go to sleep.

A prayer during ghost hunting

"Dear Heavenly Father, our loving Creator, the Source of all that is good and holy,

I thank you with all of my love for the blessing of being able to experience this earth life and all the interesting activities humans can do. I am going to ghost hunt for the express purpose of learning more about the spirit world and disembodied spirits. I do not wish to cause them harm or distress. I only wish to encounter them to experience evidence of other dimensions and to spread this information to those who will benefit from it.

In the name of the Christ and all that is good and holy. Amen."

You should repeat this prayer every time you set out on another ghost hunt but not necessarily during the same ghost hunt. Keep your vibration high during your ghost hunt.

A prayer during exorcism

"Dear Heavenly Father, our loving Creator, the Source of all that is good and holy,

I thank you with all of my love for the blessing of life. I thank you for the blessing of this person [state name]. We love you and we love each other eternally.

{State name of person] has been infected by negative spirit. We need Thy help. Please send Your legions of holy angels, even Jesus Christ and Michael the Archangel whom You love, to do battle for us and for the soul of {state name of person]. Please command the evil to release him/her and go back from whence they came even to the outer darkness.

We have every hope that this person can be a force of good for Thy purposes and the higher good of all mankind. Please be with us and cast out the devil as You can do so easily with Thy Perfect Love and Divine Power!

In the name of the Christ and all that is good and holy. Amen."

Then, directly aloud:

"IN THE NAME OF THE DOMINUS DEI, THE ALMIGHT GOD, AND JESUS CHRIST, I command you and all the negative spirits LEAVE THIS PERSON'S MIND, BODY AND SOUL. LEAVE HIM/HER NOW! DEPART AND NEVER RETURN. I COMMAND YOU TO GO BACK TO THE OUTER DARKNESS, in the name of Jesus Christ and the Almighty God of the Universe, the Alpha and the Omega, Dominus Dei, the Divine Master."

Repeat the command. You do not need to repeat the prayer as it will have been imprinted upon the positive flow of energy but negative spirit can resist so do repeat the *command* often with courage and conviction and belief.

If you hear conversation and challenges from negative spirit, do not reply. Simply repeat the command over and over.

A prayer to send a ghost spirit into the light

"Dear Heavenly Father, our loving Creator, the Source of all that is good and holy,

I thank you with all of my love for the blessing of our beloved soul brothers and sisters. We are grateful for having had the opportunity to experience life and we know that death is but a portal to eternal life.

Some of our dear departed brothers and sisters have forgotten that they are part of the Divine and there is more to their lives than just earth. Please bless them to move on. Please bless spiritual guides to come and help usher them into the light and the glorious spiritual progression that awaits them.

Please protect them from harm by evil and negative spirits. Please encircle them with Your love and protection so negativity cannot enter their vulnerable minds and confuse them. Bless them to heed the loving help they receive!

In the name of the Christ and all that is good and holy. Amen."

Then, directly aloud:

"Greetings. Please do not be afraid. I have a message for you. You may or may not recognize that you are no longer in your physical body. You have died. But your spirit form is eternal which is why you still believe you are alive on earth. It is time for you to move onto your next spiritual existence. No matter what you may believe, goodness and love await you. No matter what you may have done here on earth, there is more to learn and you will continue learning.

Please go and be at peace. Enter the light of love and wellness. When gentle and loving persons come to you, trust them and heed their guidance. If you feel confused and cannot tell between a good or evil person, simply ask yourself if you feel true peace emanating from him or her. Do you feel a pervasive all-loving presence?

Can you choose to stay in your present condition? You can remain earthbound but you can't stay here in this abode. You must leave it. Know there is more joy than you can imagine if you but trust enough to enter the light. You will be happy once again. I say these things to you in the name of Jesus Christ and the Almighty God of the Universe, the Alpha and the Omega, Dominus Dei, the Divine Master."

About helping ghosts cross over

People have the good intention of "saving" souls or sending them into the light so they will no longer be earthbound. However, there are a few considerations to know.

1. Not all spirits will cross over. They still can exercise their free will to stay earthbound, and some do not want to cross over for a various reasons. Some fear the unknown. Some fear what they think will be their retribution or punishment for misdeeds. Others do not want to let go on their earth lives. Some stay to fulfill some task they believe they must.

2. Not all spirits can cross over. Spirits who never lived will not be able to go into the light at this time. Their hour of 'redemption' will come at a later time. However, they can be sent away from you.

3. Do not allow your compassion to keep you in dark places. Feel at peace because there are helpful guides at work here and on the other side who are working to gather the lost and confused. Some people are born with specific gifts to be used to aid them. Unless you have a clear calling to join the cause, don't fall into the trap of staying in lower vibrational places because you feel sorry for ghosts.

This book largely concerns itself with protection from evil spirit energy. Dealing with ghosts are another matter for another book.

ABOUT THE AUTHOR

Lori Phillips writes about spirituality, dream interpretation, and relationships. She considers herself inter-faith with respect for all. Her explorations of religious denominations, including multi-cultural, Asian, Christian, and metaphysical thought, have aided her during own personal experiences with the paranormal. She assists both the living and the dead.

Her academic credits include a master of education (M.Ed) and bachelor's degrees in both communications and metaphysical sciences. She is working on her doctorate in the latter.

She lives in Southern California with her family and three Chihuahua mixes, all who remain safe and protected albeit a bit flummoxed by the occasional passing spirit.

Made in the USA
Monee, IL
19 March 2021

63307778R20036